CAROLYN J. SMITH

WESTBOW
PRESS®
A DIVISION OF THOMAS NELSON
& ZONDERVAN

WestBow Press books may be ordered through booksellers or by contacting:

WestBow Press
A Division of Thomas Nelson & Zondervan
1663 Liberty Drive
Bloomington, IN 47403
www.westbowpress.com
844-714-3454

ISBN: 978-1-6642-0622-9 (sc)
ISBN: 978-1-6642-0623-6 (e)

Print information available on the last page.

WestBow Press rev. date: 10/28/2020

Dedication

I dedicate this book to my entire family in appreciation for the love and support they show each other. We may not always agree, and we do have our differences, but when we come together those differences are put aside.

As of this year, (2020) we have 143 members in the family tree from the union of Llewellyn (Hap) and Virginia (Ginge) Smith. They both left an indelible and Godly mark in each of our lives.

Acknowledgement

I want to give my heartful thanks to Lisa, my dear friend Gerda's daughter. I appreciate her dedication. She spent many hours helping to ensure that my message was clear and my goal to honor my Mom was met.

Thank you, Lisa, for your belief in me, as a writer and your constant encouragement for me to improve my craft.

Foreword

As the oldest grandchild of Virginia Smith, I often heard her say, "Everyone looking at me can tell I am a new Grandma." She said this each time a new grandchild arrived, and she had 23 biological grandkids plus many that were "chosen" to be grandchildren by her. Virginia simply adored the role of Grandma.

Being the first-born and "oldest" cousin, a special bond formed between my Grandmother and me. We always had our "secret and special" times just for us. I still treasure those times and always will. In those moments, I gleaned from her - her wisdom, her deep love for her Savior, her husband, her family, and all those whom God placed in her life.

She shared with me her love for games and puzzles, music and singing, being silly, and listening for God's voice. Thinking back over her life, although I want to believe that I was the only one, truth is - she probably had "secret and special" times with all her grandchildren.

There has always been an on-going friendly rivalry among the cousins about who was Grandma's favorite grandchild. Well, sorry cousins, I was without a doubt her favorite.

Shari Smith Walters
Virginia Smith's Oldest and Favorite Grandchild

Contents

Preface xiii

The Early Years 1
The Great Loss 3
Romance 5
Family Creation 7
Weekly Responsibilities 9
Faith 13
Sorrow 17
Family Life 19
Care Giving 27
Empty Nesters and Comical Antidotes 29
Farewell 33
Family Reunions 35
Assisted Living 39
Nursing Home 41
Smith Family Singers 47
Compassion 51
Pearls of Wisdom 53
Going Home 55

Epilogue 59

Preface

Who was this woman who had a difficult life, but found such joy in everything she did, always finding something positive in every situation. Though at times, she cried, mourned, felt angry, or felt sorry for herself; she always managed to find humor in life's experiences.

She was a respectful and precocious child, a loving and caring wife, an involved and compassionate mother to eight children, grandma to 23 grandchildren, a great-grandmother to many, and a devoted, entertaining friend.

Virginia Sweet Smith, dealt with her difficulties, performed her tasks wholeheartedly, and genuinely enjoyed her life that was chocked-full of experiences.

"Shout for joy to the Lord, all the earth, burst into jubilant song with music." Psalm 98:4 NIV

The Early Years

On July 22, 1913, Virginia Sweet was born to Guy Gilbert and Ella Vern Sweet. The parents were elated with their little girl. Guy adored his daughter and learned early on that she was an engaging, entertaining, and mischievous child. The two of them were great pals who loved cooking up pranks to pull on anyone, especially Ella, who was always focused on the details of life and rarely took time to sit back and have fun.

Guy wanted to be the best dad that he could be and strove to make every day special for his daughter. He particularly wanted Christmas to be exceptional. One Christmas Eve when Virginia was about four, she heard heavy footsteps galumphing down the attic stairs that were in her room. Her immediate reaction was fear. As the figure entered her room, Virginia saw that it was Santa Claus, and in his arms was a chair, just her size. What a delightful and enchanting experience for a little girl. Virginia only found out many years later that Santa had been her dad and that he had built the chair for her.

As she grew older, Virginia's father included her in many of the pranks that he pulled on his wife Ella. The shenanigans always annoyed Ella, and that was what Guy enjoyed the most. Ella's personality was so different from that of Guy and Virginia. One night while Ella was busy preparing dinner, Guy and Virginia hid some limburger cheese in a plate of food and set it in the middle of the table. When they all were at the table eating dinner, Ella noticed that something smelled horrible, even though the food tasted delicious. She made comments about the odor and Virginia and her dad had to work extremely hard to hide their amusement. When Ella finally discovered the source of the smell, she knew immediately who was responsible. She was not pleased with these two and reacted exactly as they had hoped. Guy and Virginia felt that their prank had been a huge success.

Life for Virginia was perfect. She lived on a quiet tree-lined street in Jackson, Michigan. She started wearing glasses at age three and endured the mean comments of others. Virginia learned to foster friendships with people who did not ridicule her. She was a fun friend who could always be counted on to stir up some excitement.

(Virginia (in white) with her pals eating ice cream.)

The Great Loss

Suddenly at the age of 12, life as she knew it came to a halt when Virginia's father unexpectedly died. Guy worked as a grinder in a factory. In this era, the 1920s, there were no requirements for workers' safety equipment. Each day while performing his job, Guy breathed in the tiny particles from the grinder. Upon his death it was determined that these particles had entered his brain and caused his untimely death. The glasses that Guy wore daily were pitted from particles.

Virginia and Ella were devastated. Their lives changed dramatically. Ella needed to find a way to support herself and her daughter. A quick way to generate income was to take in borders. The house they lived in had three bedrooms and one bath. Ella figured she and Virginia could share a room which would leave two rooms available for rent. Ella loved to cook so feeding the borders would not be a problem. Soon, however, Ella realized that the income from the boarders was not going to completely sustain them, and that she needed to find a job. Ella was an honest, hardworking, ethical person and was able to secure a job quickly.

VIRGINIA (LEFT) AS A
TEEN WITH ELLA.

Each day when Ella went off to work, she left a list of chores for Virginia to complete. A fun and resourceful kid, Virginia played all day with her friends and then about an hour before her Mom was due to arrive home, she would recruit her friends to help with her chores. When Ella arrived home, all was in order and she was never the wiser.

Romance

At 17, Virginia accepted an invitation to go on a blind date with a handsome young man, two years older than she, who had been raised in the small farming town of Munith, Michigan. Llewellyn Smith and Virginia went to a blind pig with another couple, where they danced, laughed, and had a great time. Llewellyn and Virginia enjoyed each other's company so much that they continued to date, and Virginia always said, "I was blind ever after."

They were a perfect couple. Both were witty, loved to laugh and joke around. Neither of them took life too seriously.

Llewellyn's friends called him "Hap," which was short for Happy Hooligan. Hap fondly began to call Virginia "Ginge."

Their relationship blossomed into a love affair that lasted 51 years. Hap reminded Ginge of her father with his practical jokes and sense of humor. She could not help but fall in love with him.

Because of the Great Depression, Hap and Ginge had a small wedding with just

LLEWELLYN AS A YOUNG MAN.

family on Christmas Eve, 1931 at St. Paul's Lutheran Church in Jackson. After the ceremony they drove to Battle Creek to pick up

Ginge's Aunt so she could spend Christmas Day with them. They never did go on a honeymoon and Hap continuously said that Virginia was his Christmas present which he was still paying for.

⚬

Just before the wedding, one of Ella's boarders had purchased an 80-acre farm in Battle Creek and asked her to come live there to cook and keep house for him. Ella moved to the farm and gave her house in Jackson, Michigan to Hap and Ginge. Now they had a place to live, Hap and Ginge got busy filling the house with lots of noisy, unruly, and adored children.

Family Creation

When Ginge became pregnant with the first of her eight children she was excited. She eagerly anticipated a warm and homey environment for her family. The years her Mother had worked and delegated household chores to Ginge had prepared her well. Ginge embraced the responsibilities of young married life. Cooking, cleaning, laundry, and ironing were tasks she accepted willingly. She rose every day at 5:30 am to prepare breakfast for Hap and fix a lunch for him to take to his job as a Tool and Die Maker.

While preparing Hap's breakfast she could be heard singing opera or show tunes. She had a beautiful soprano voice, adored music, and loved to sing at any time of the day or night. Even though she might have been up all night, her cheerful personality always kicked in and allowed her to live her daily life with delight, exploding with exuberance.

The babies arrived at regular intervals and Ginge gained more love than she thought possible. First came Ronnie (1932), then Jerry (1934), Gloria (1935), Darlene (1937), Margaret Ann (1941), Carolyn (1942), Sandra (1944) and Dianne (1946). Each child was unique, and she loved them unconditionally. As they grew older and started school she would stand at the bottom of the stairs and sing out, "Get up, get up, get up! Today's the day they give babies away with a half a pound of tea."

As each child got out of bed and dressed for school, Ginge, back in the kitchen, was making hot cereal for their breakfast and fixing their lunches. A couple of the kids did not wake up in a good mood and it was difficult for them to listen to Ginge with her "happy go lucky" attitude. She would not let them spoil her mood and they soon accepted that she would not change. What was so amazing about this joy she possessed was the fact that she had many reasons not to be joyful. She had a packed schedule to accomplish each day of the week.

Weekly Responsibilities

Monday was laundry day. Ginge used a wringer washing machine. Because clothes dryers had not yet been invented, she either hung the clothes on the line outside or in the winter, draped them over small racks and chairs on the inside of the house. She would often stand at the back door and admired how white her sheets were. She took pride in what she accomplished.

On Tuesdays she prepared the clothes for ironing. She used a sprinkle cork inserted into an empty coke bottle to wet the clothes, rolled them up, and put them in the wicker ironing basket. If it were summer and hot, she would put the sprinkled clothes in the refrigerator so they would not mildew.

SPRINKLING BOTTLE

Wednesdays and Thursdays were entirely devoted to ironing the clothes for all nine members of the family. In those days permanent press material did not exist. The kids would generally wear school clothes two days in a row, changing into play clothes after school. Everyone would have something nice to wear to church on Sunday.

On Friday while the children were in school Ginge cleaned

the three bedrooms and bathroom. Working alone she sang to her heart's content and had ample opportunity to admire her work.

Saturdays the entire family pitched in to clean the living room, dining room, kitchen, and mop and vacuum all the floors. Saturday was also grocery shopping day. Ginge and Hap would go to the grocery store together. The budget was $15. 00 a week.

However, Ginge had a fruit cellar loaded with canned meat, vegetables, and fruit. All they needed to buy was bread and other essentials, like a bunch of bananas. The bananas did not last long so if you wanted one, you had to be sure and get one on Saturday, because by Sunday they were gone.

Milk was delivered twice a week to the house. The milkman left three or four glass bottles of milk on the porch. During the winter months, the milk needed to

FRUIT CELLAR

be brought in soon. Otherwise, the milk would freeze, and the glass bottles would break. Sometimes, they would remember to retrieve the milk just before the breaking point, but the cream had already separated, risen to the top and exploded through the cardboard covering.

After dinner on Saturday, while Ginge was cleaning up the kitchen, Hap and Gloria gave the younger children their weekly bath. While the bathing was taking place, Ginge made fudge and popcorn. When all were bathed and ready for bed, it was treat-time. They gathered around the radio and listened to *"Gang Busters."* This was the highlight of the week and everyone from the oldest to the youngest looked forward to this show with anticipation.

Sundays were a day of rest; but not for Ginge. She would fix breakfast for Hap, then get the kids up and fix their breakfast.

Then she began to put the mid-day meal together so that it would be ready when they returned from church. It was usually a pot roast with mashed potatoes and gravy, and a vegetable. While she was doing all of this, Hap read the Sunday paper and then went upstairs to get ready for church. He always had "first dibs" on the only bathroom.

By the time Hap and the eight kids were ready for church Ginge had just finished in the kitchen and now it was her turn to get herself ready. The problem was that by now Hap was sitting in the car with the kids, motor running, and honking the horn for Ginge to join them.

Once or twice a year, Hap and Ginge would invite a visiting pastor to join the family for lunch. On these occasions, Ginge worked extra hard at preparing the meal which always included a homemade pie. In addition to the regular Sunday morning chaos, the pressure of a perfect mid-day meal was added to her shoulders.

Company or no company, discipline was maintained. One Sunday, a child used a word that was unacceptable. Ginge stopped what she was doing, sat the child on a stool in the kitchen with a bar of soap in her mouth. She did not make a big deal out of it and our guests had no idea it had happened. I know this is true because that child was me.

Faith

Through their children, Hap and Ginge became good friends with their neighbors. A neighbor couple, Ima and Tuck, invited Hap and Ginge along with their children to attend a service at the Baptist Church. Hap and Ginge not only attended regularly, they and their children were saved, baptized, and joined this church. Within a couple of years of attendance Hap was asked to sit on the Church Board, and Ginge was singing in the choir and teaching Sunday School. Life was good. Church was a place they could grow their faith, be involved in social activities, and make friends. It did not create a financial burden.

Ten years after joining the Baptist church, Ginge was invited to attend a women's weekly Bible Study by a different neighbor, Opal who attended a Pentecostal Church. All but one of the kids were in school which meant she had the time to join. While attending this Bible Study, Ginge felt God's Presence in a way that she never had before. After attending these Bible Studies, Sunday service at her own Baptist Church was never quite the same.

Ginge started going to the Wednesday night services at the Pentecostal Church and took her oldest teenage daughter, Gloria, with her. After hearing the Pentecostal Youth Pastor speak, Gloria, who oversaw the Baptist Youth Group invited him to speak at their church.

The Baptist Pastor was not happy about this incident. Instead of going to Hap and Ginge privately to discuss it with them, he declared from the pulpit, "Llewellyn, you need to have better control of your wife." Ginge's first reaction was embarrassment. Hap's was anger. He stood up at the end of the pew where the family was sitting, and announced, "Come, we are leaving." With that declaration, the entire Smith family marched out of the Baptist Church, never to attend again.

The next Sunday the entire Smith family filed into the Pentecostal Church. Here again, Hap was asked to sit on the Board and Ginge taught Sunday School. She made some good friends, like Lillian, Adele, Beechey, Purdy and Helen. Ginge and Helen were two of a kind with their quick wit and managed to always be laughing about something. Everyone wanted to be friends with them because they were so much fun to be around. Their laughter was contagious.

Ginge's weekly morning routine changed significantly. After Hap left for work, she had about a half an hour before she had to wake up the kids. She took this opportunity to read her Bible and pray. She could be heard praying for her children. Speaking their names out loud and praying a specific prayer for each one. When she was finished praying, she stood at the bottom of the stairs and gave out her daily wakeup call, "Get up, get up, get up! Today's the day they give babies away with a half a pound of tea."

Ginge's obedience to the Holy Spirit in acknowledging God's Presence in her life was significant to the Smith family. Because of her faithfulness, all her children developed a personal relationship with Christ. Gloria graduated from Bible College, got

CAROLYN IN UGANDA

married and with her husband they became missionaries in Africa. Darlene married a Pastor and later served as a missionary in Great Britain. Ronnie and his wife made several mission trips to Mexico, and Carolyn went with a mission group to Uganda. Many of Ginge's grandchildren and great-grandchildren have also been on mission trips. One may say that the fruit of Ginge's obedience stretched throughout the world.

"So, the word of God spread. The number of disciples in Jerusalem increased rapidly, and a large number of priests became obedient to the faith." Act 6:7 NIV

Sorrow

By 1941, Ginge had five kids to take care of, and life was good. They were happy within their family and through their church family. Then sorrow struck the entire Smith clan.

Close to a year after daughter Margaret Ann was born, Ginge realized that the baby was not feeling well. She was lethargic, her skin was pale, and the rosy cheeks she had six months earlier were gone. Ginge could not get her to eat and was so worried, that she asked her church family to pray for Margaret Ann.

When Margaret Ann's condition worsened, Ginge took her to one doctor after another. No one could determine what was wrong with her. It was suggested that Margaret Ann be admitted to the

FAMILY WITH MARGARET ANN

hospital for testing. It broke Ginge's heart to leave her baby girl all alone in the hospital. Before leaving, Hap donated blood in case Margaret Ann needed it. Hap and Ginge returned home to care for the rest of the family. While they were eating dinner, the hospital called to say there was a big change in Margaret

Ann's condition and they should return to the hospital as soon as possible. By the time Hap and Ginge arrived, Margaret Ann had died. An autopsy determined that Margaret Ann had suffered from leukemia.

When Hap informed the family of her death, they were all in shock and denial that this could happen to their sweet delightful and fun baby sister whom they adored.

⚜

With a new dress, new socks, and new shoes Margaret Ann was laid out in a casket in the living room. Visitation lasted three days. The many people coming into the home provided support through this unbelievable sadness.

Darlene who was only four years old did not fully understand what was going on. She thought that if she died, she would get some new shoes too, like Margaret Ann.

Burying her baby and striving to stay strong for the other children, Ginge discovered that she was pregnant again. She did not feel she could tell anyone, but within her being she knew that God loved her and Margaret Ann, yet He had another plan for them. She held fast to the scripture below:

"For I know the plans I have for you."
declares the Lord, "plans to prosper you
and not to harm you, plans to give you
hope and a future." Jeremiah 29:11 NIV

Family Life

With the births of Carolyn (me), Sandy, and Dianne the family returned to a more normal existence. Mom was now caring for eight people and living in her childhood home on Pleasant Street. We were a noisy bunch and like most siblings we quarreled. It was hard for Mom to understand why we argued so much. She would always remind us of how lonely she had been growing up, while we had all these siblings to play with, yet we quarreled.

The family had quite the reputation among the neighbors. We were the only house on Pleasant Street without grass in the front yard. The continuous activity going on in there wiped away any grass that struggled to grow. The lack of grass was not at the top of the "worry" list for Dad and Mom, it was not only due to the Smith kids, but also their friends. The Smith house was where all the racket came from; during the day, but also after dark, when a game of "kick the can" or "hide n seek" took place. Everyone knew if your child was absent, check out the Smith home.

Mom's workload slowly eased as the kids got older. Gloria was especially helpful with the younger kids. Mom still did all the cooking, but we all pitched in to set the dining room table, fill the water glasses (milk was only served at breakfast), clear the table, and do the dishes. There were very few times that someone did not knock over their water glass during dinner which interrupted the meal until the water was mopped up, and Dad bellowed out, "Does someone always have to spill their water every night?" After dinner was over, Mom finally had time to read the paper or sit on the front porch and relax. This was her favorite part of the day.

Every time Mom was preparing hamburger for dinner, she could be seen taking a pinch of the raw burger, rolling it into a ball, sprinkling a little salt and pepper on it, and popping it into her mouth. She loved this snack, and no matter what people said about eating raw meat, she continued the habit. Other times when she wanted an afternoon snack, she took a slice of bread, spread butter on it, then catsup, folded it in half and ate it.

Ketchup was always on hand in the Smith cupboards. As a matter of fact, once Dad purchased five bottles at a time as he wanted to compete in a contest that required five ketchup labels to enter. The $500 prize was the subject of conversation at the dinner table. This was a fun time for the entire family, and for a moment took us to another place. Dad was a dreamer and he taught his children the art of dreaming big.

When Scarlet Fever spread throughout the United States, the Smith family did not escape this virus. Mom never contracted it, but almost everyone else in the household did. At the first declaration that one of the children had the disease, the Jackson Health Department came to Pleasant Street and nailed a quarantine sign on the front door. Mom was great at taking care of the sick child as well as everyone else. As soon as one child recovered, another one would come down with it. She could not go out of the house for at least four weeks. Dad could go to work every day so that we could afford food.

When all the children had finally cleared the disease, the Health Department came in the morning and took down the sign. They returned later that same day to put the sign back up, because Dad had been diagnosed with the disease. The fact that Dad was not able to go to work, put the Smith family into a difficult position regarding having enough money for food. The Health Department brought a box full of food and left it on the back porch to help us out. This was the only time, Dad and Mom ever took any type of government aid. Dad was too proud to take handouts.

There was a time when Dad was voted to be the President of his local UAW/CIO union. This position required him to be gone a great amount of time. Though Mom was unhappy about it, they did not quarrel in front of us. She missed him. When Dad returned home, he was tired after working all day, and then being in union meetings until late in the evening. Dad's tenure as President was three to four years and when it was over, there was no one happier than Mom. She had her man back.

This difficult period did, however, yield a proud moment for Mom and the rest of us. The company that Dad worked for made sonar buoys used by the United States Navy to detect enemy submarines during WWII. A couple of years after the war, as President of this union, he was honored to accept an award on behalf of the union from the Navy, thanking the union for their war efforts.

❧❦☙

Dad loved to eat. During the season, he brought home bushels of fresh tomatoes, beans, peaches, pears, etc. He did not expect Mom to can these by herself, he also pitched in. The fruit cellar in the basement had three sides with shelves that were stocked full of fruit, vegetables, and meat to make sure that we had healthy dinners in the winter as well as in the summer.

Occasionally, someone would give us a live chicken or a dead squirrel. Dad and Mom went to the basement to prepare the

HAP WITH A TURKEY LEG & GINGE

animal. Mom was incredibly supportive in this endeavor. When the chicken was dead, she brought down the kettle of boiling water to help pluck the feathers off the chicken or to help skin the squirrel. She never complained, but rather looked forward to the meal she would prepare with these meats.

One dish that Mom made quite often required a lot of preparation time. She called it "city chicken." This dish was truly a labor of love. She often made it for Sunday's mid-day meal. The preparations began on Saturday; she took wooden skewers and placed small chunks of chicken, pork, and beef until each skewer was full. She dipped the full skewer into egg, rolled it in breadcrumbs and browned it in a cast iron skillet. As each skewer was crispy, she placed it in the turkey roasting pan. Sunday

Carolyn J. Smith

morning before we left for church, she put the roasting pan into the oven to cook slowly. When we returned home from church, they were ready to eat. To feed our family, Mom prepared 30 to 40 skewers of her "city chicken."

Another activity that Mom and Dad did together was making homemade ice cream. Mom would stand at the stove and cook the yummy ingredients; eggs, cream, and vanilla until it was just the right consistency. She then gave this mixture to Dad who placed it in a metal canister that sat in the middle of a wooden container filled with ice. Once he had the top on and the metal canister locked in place, he began to turn the crank. This was a family affair, as everyone took a turn on the crank. Dad could tell when the mixture was frozen and removed the metal canister and dished up the ice cream. Everyone loved it and applauded Dad. Even though Mom had created the mixture, she never felt slighted about not receiving any praises. Watching everyone enjoy this treat was reward enough for her.

There was always something unusual taking place in our home on Pleasant Street. Once there was a bat in one of the bedrooms, which was a particularly exciting and scary event. We all wanted to watch Dad catch the bat and joined him in the bedroom. Dad swung the broom at the bat and missed; the bat started to fly around. Everyone was bending over and ducking their heads. Mom was not so fortunate. The bat landed on her head and became tangled in her hair. With that, she let out a loud and high-pitched scream, at the same time relieving herself. There she stood screaming with the bat on her head and a puddle at her feet. Dad was able to remove the bat from her hair quickly and disposed of it. As things quieted down, the rest of the evening was filled with conversation from each of us kids about how this event affected us. For me, it left me with a fear of anything that flies.

One day Gloria wanted to help Mom by learning how to use the wringer washing machine. Mom sat on the cellar steps giving careful instructions to make sure that Gloria did not get hurt. Once the clothes were in the machine, the wringer was moving back and forth, a three-foot stick was used to push down the clothes so they would all be mixed in with the soapy water. Gloria got the stick, when she pushed down the clothes, the stick hit the wringer and it went flying out of her hands and into the air. It hit Mom on the legs. After the sting from the stick wore off, both Mom and Gloria could not stop laughing. I am not sure if Mom ever let Gloria do the laundry again.

Our family was very musical. This gift was inherited from Mom. When each of us reached junior high school, we were given the opportunity to learn to play an instrument. Mom let us make our own choice and never knew which instrument any of us would choose.

Jerry decided that he was going to be in the band. Mom was sitting on our front porch waiting for everyone to arrive home from school, when she looked up and turning the corner onto Pleasant Street was Jerry carrying a huge tuba. He was so skinny that the instrument overpowered him. Mom was amazed that he was able to carry it. He was so proud of himself and Mom encouraged his decision even though she was flabbergasted.

Gloria, Darlene, and I all took piano lessons. We had an upright piano in the living room where we could practice. Gloria and Darlene continued with the lessons longer than I, and both became proficient. Darlene had a tremendous gift of being able to play by ear. When I wanted to sing a solo at church, I would learn the song, sing it to her, and she would accompany me in the key that was comfortable for me to sing in.

When I reached junior high, I elected to play the flute. but my first love was singing.

Sandy chose the saxophone and would play it throughout the house. I don't remember how good she sounded, but I do remember that one night after dinner, she and Darlene got into a argument. Sandy lost her temper, and hit Darlene over the head with her saxophone. Of course, Mom and Dad had to pay for the repair, which was not easy on an already tight budget.

SUNDAY DINNER WITH THE ENTIRE SMITH FAMILY INCLUDING ELLA (GRANDMA) SWEET AND LAWRENCE (GRANDPA) SMITH

Dianne decided she would play the violin. Of all the instruments that came through our house, this one was the most difficult to listen to while she practiced. Even Mom had difficulty listening to the screeching coming from the violin.

Care Giving

With three young teenagers still in the house, Mom took on the care of Grandpa Smith, who after some major surgery was not immediately able to return to his home. He had been a hardworking farmer all his life and did not really know how to have fun. He believed that every minute of the day should be productive. To sit and read a book or watch TV was a waste of time.

When Sandy, Dianne and I would come home from school, the first thing we did was to watch *American Bandstand*. This used to drive Grandpa nuts. He thought all those kids on TV should be out delivering newspapers rather than dancing on a show, and that included us. We ignored the comments from Grandpa Smith and privately were happy when he was well enough to go back home.

Later, Grandma Sweet came to live with us. She had been living on the farm in Battle Creek since 1931, but events occurred that led her to come back to Jackson and moved in with us. Grandma's attitude toward leisure was not much different from Grandpa Smith, but we all knew that we had to show her respect.

Life got a little harder for Mom when Grandma fell and broke her hip. We had to install a hospital bed in our living room for Grandma, as she was not able to climb the stairs. Mom had to help Grandma with a bed pan, bathe her, feed her, and keep her as comfortable as possible. Despite Mom's efforts, Grandma developed pneumonia and died.

A few years after Grandma died, her brother, Uncle Webb asked if he could come to live with my parents. They agreed.

My Mom and Dad believed that the act of caring for someone is what the Bible teaches us to do, i.e., to follow the Good Samaritan parable. During the care of all these family members, my Mother never complained. She undertook this task with a willing heart and found joy in serving.

"But a Samaritan, as he traveled, came where the man was; and when he saw him, he took pity on him. He went to him and bandaged his wounds, pouring on oil and wine. Then he put the man on his own donkey, took him to an inn and took care of him." Luke 10:33-34 NIV

Empty Nesters and Comical Antidotes

As each child, one after the other, finished high school and left home, Ginge's responsibilities lessened. Though her children were adults, she still worried about them and continued to pray every day for each child and his or her family. Her morning routine became easier and allowed her more time in her Bible and prayer.

SOME OF THE SMITH GRANDCHILDREN AND GREAT-GRANDCHILDREN.

Grandchildren started arriving. Ginge loved them all. She had a unique way of making each one feel that they were her favorite. Ginge enjoyed having her grandchildren around and found them entertaining. She enjoyed them mainly because she did not have to raise them. After having a fun time, her grandchildren returned home to their parents.

One of her favorite things to do was to have a few grandkids visit and play cribbage or other card games. Hap got a little jealous sometimes, as Ginge was showing more attention to the grandkids than to him. She was mindful of this and had her own way of appeasing him.

As her kids continued to produce more grandchildren, Ginge created a "hard and fast rule." She would not babysit so the parents could go to work every day or go out and have fun. This did not mean, however, that if there were an emergency, she could not amend her rule. She realized early on that babysitting grandchildren could cause problems with her own kids if she babysat more for one family than the other. This rule was self-preservation on her part.

The grandchildren loved being around Ginge. She encouraged them in mischievous behavior just as her father had done with her. She was the first one to laugh at herself and never felt bad when others laughed along with her.

Ginge especially enjoyed being invited to her children's houses for dinner and visiting grandchildren. She could enjoy herself with her kids and grandkids and did not have to be responsible for dinner or clean up.

The birth dates of every one of the 23 grandchildren were extremely important to her. She had memorized the birth dates of each one and made sure to send them a birthday card and always included a one-dollar bill. Receiving the card and money was exciting for each grandchild. They thought they had received an abundance of money. She continued this practice until they became teenagers and she no longer had the funds to send them. She did, however, enlist the help of others to continue sending her children birthday cards.

⁊───∞───⁊

Dianne had an above the ground pool in her back yard. One hot summer day she invited Sandy and I to bring Mom along with our own children and go swimming. Mom loved the water and enjoyed swimming and playing with all of us. The time came to get out and dry off. Everyone got out of the pool except Mom. She did not have the strength to pull herself out of the pool. Sandy and I got on the outside and pulled on her arms, while Dianne and the grandkids stayed in the pool to push on her bottom to help get her out. This was quite an achievement, since we were all laughing so hard.

⁊───∞───⁊

Mom was able to spend a day with her friends, Opal, Lillian, Adele and Beechy. They were at the lake, to have lunch and go for a boat ride. While trying to step onto the boat, Mom slipped on the dock and cut her leg seriously. Her injury was so severe they had to call an ambulance. She became upset when in the E.R. they announced they would have to cut off her girdle, exclaiming, "This is brand new and I can't afford to buy another one." The nurses expressed their sympathy, but it was the only way to treat her. For days afterwards, Ginge was upset about her new, now gone, girdle.

⁊───∞───⁊

Dad and Mom asked me to drive them to New York so they could spend Easter with Gloria and her family. I was not married at the time and decided I would also like to see my sister and her family.

When we got to New York, Gloria wanted to treat Mom and I to a "spa day" at a health center. We enjoyed the amazing hot tub for about 30 minutes.

Gloria and I stood up to climb the few steps out of the tub, but Mom could barely stand and had no strength to lift her legs onto the steps. We practically carried her to the locker room where she sat like a blob on the wooden bench; her arms hanging lifeless at her sides. She looked like a rag doll and we started to giggle and then the full-on laughter started and was infectious. Mom laughed along with us. She loved the attention she was getting from both us.

When we returned to Gloria's house, we were still laughing about what had occurred. Gloria's daughter, who is a nurse, happened to be there and scolded us about the gravity of the situation and what could have happened to Mom. We did not realize that due to Mom's blood pressure issues, we should have taken her out after about ten minutes. We were unaware of the seriousness of her condition. We felt a little contrite but could not stop seeing the humor in the day we had just experienced.

❦

Farewell

After Dad retired, my parents moved out of the house on Pleasant Street into a small bungalow in Jackson. This was easier for them as there were no stairs to climb and not a big area to clean.

On May 5, 1984, Dad and Mom went out to dinner with his brother and cousin and their wives, which was something they did about once a month. After dinner they returned to Mom and Dad's house to continue visiting and posed for a picture of all of them in front of the house.

When everyone left, Dad told Mom that he was not feeling well and went to lay down and listen to the Tiger's baseball game. Mom was not alarmed by this behavior as he did it often; he was a huge Tigers fan. A short time later, Mom heard a large thud, went into the bedroom, and found Dad on the floor. He had had a massive heart attack and died. It was a wonderful way to die - doing what he loved, listening to a Tiger game. Fittingly, the Tigers were playing the Angels (LA) that day.

MOM AND DAD WITH RELATIVES
AND DAISY THE DOG.

What followed was extremely sad for Mom as well as for the rest of us. During their time together, Dad had made all the decisions. Now Mom would be making her own choices. Several years after Dad had died, Mom told me, "Don't misunderstand me, I do miss your Dad terribly, however, I like making my own decisions." She had become a 20th century woman and was enjoying it.

⁕

During the visitation at the funeral home, there were many old friends from Mom and Dad, and the rest of the family. What surprised us all was the visits from neighbors that grew up in our neighborhood. His visitations became a party-like atmosphere and we realized we needed to tone it down as there were other people in the funeral home that were also grieving. Dad would have loved the fact that we were laughing and enjoying the visitors.

At his funeral, three pastors spoke, along with his children, grandchildren, and friends. One tribute that continues to stand out for me was from Rev. Robert (Bob) Norman. Bob told a story about how diligent Dad had been as a Sunday school teacher. Each week Dad came prepared to teach the lesson with knowledge and enthusiasm. He taught as if speaking to a room full of young boys, but in fact there was only one, and it was Bob.

Family Reunions

Acouple of years after Dad died, we started gathering at my house in July, to celebrate Mom's birthday. At that time, I lived on six acres with a pond. Everyone would come to Ann Arbor; Ronnie and his family travelled from Battle Creek; Jerry, Darlene, Sandy, and Dianne came along with their families from Jackson; Gloria and her family came from New York and Virginia; and my children came with their families from Chelsea and Oregon. Most everyone arrived on Saturday around noon. While the adults set up their tents or motorhomes, the kids were in the pond swimming, fishing or on the paddle boat. We all looked forward to this event, especially Mom, as she was the main attraction.

We had enough family members to have two teams for a game of baseball. It was quite hilarious! From those of us who could still hit the ball but had difficulty running the bases, to the little ones that needed assistance to bat the ball. When the little kids were up to bat, the fielders deliberately fumbled the ball so many times they were able to get a homerun. In addition to those who were in the game, we still had enough family members left over for a cheering section.

During the entire weekend, a karaoke machine was set up on the deck and anyone, young or old, was able to use it. When the spirit moved someone, they would find the tape music they wanted, grab the microphone and sing.

On Saturday after dinner and when darkness fell, we built a bonfire by the pond and roasted marshmallows for "smores." The men would set up fireworks out in the field.

The best fireworks ever were the ones that we had for Mom's 90th birthday celebration. For her 90th we created special  invitations and invited many of her old friends that she had not seen for years. It was gratifying to watch her communicating with them, catching up on their lives, and rehashing comical incidents that happened years ago.

On Sunday, we made a big breakfast for 80 to 90 of us. The kitchen stove and oven, the grill, and even the turkey fryer were utilized to create a feast of biscuits, toast, sausage gravy, scrambled eggs, blueberry waffles, hash browns, donuts, and fruit. One of the nieces who is a nurse referred to this breakfast as "heart attack on a plate."

After breakfast, we all gathered down by the pond; some sitting in lawn chairs and some sitting on blankets for a church service. One family member would start us with prayer, then the praise and worship team which consisted of two guitarists, a keyboard, and drums, along with two or three singers led us in worship. Mom especially enjoyed singing and worshipping with her family. After worship, we would hear a sermon from Gloria's husband who was an ordained minister.

Carolyn J. Smith

REUNION

PRAISE TEAM

DIANNE, SANDY, JERRY, MOM, RONNIE, GLORIA, CAROLYN & DARLENE

Assisted Living

Mom's friend, Opal, moved to an upscale retirement home and she wanted to move there too. It would be a place where Mom could have a lovely apartment, see Opal every day, and be around people. Interaction with people was what she loved the most and it provided a steady audience to whom she could brag about her children and grandchildren.

After about a year she had to move to a place that was a little less expensive. She fit in well here also. If she wanted to be alone or did not feel good, she could stay in her apartment. If she felt lonely, she would sit in the reception area and wait for people she knew to return from shopping or other errands. As soon as their feet hit the door, she was starting a conversation with them.

Euchre was played once a week at this retirement home. Mom absolutely loved this game and was always willing to play. However, she had a strong conviction regarding gambling. Mom felt that gambling was not something God approved of. When she agreed to join the euchre group, she did not realize that everyone had to put twenty-five cents in the pot. (In her mind, this constitutes gambling.) Ultimately, she decided she would play anyway and deposited her quarter in the pot. When she won the pot, she was able to justify her winnings, as she needed the quarters to use for her laundry.

Mom did not drive because of her age. She was always willing to go whenever anyone invited her. She often said, "Don't invite me unless you mean it, because I'm going."

Ronnie and his wife offered to include her in their vacation to Florida. She was excited to be able to go on a trip. She was no longer able to travel by herself and her friends did not drive either.

After being on the road for a while, Ronnie was hungry and stopped at a McDonald's. Once seated inside at a table, he asked Mom what she would like to eat. She told him, "Just a hamburger and a drink." He specifically asked her, "You don't want any fries to go with that?" She told him she did not. He asked her the same question once more and she again said, "No."

Ronnie ordered the food and came back with everyone's order. As he sat his hamburgers, fries, and a drink in front of him, Mom reached over and took a French fry from him. Ronnie was always calm, cool, and collected. It took a lot to irritate him. One of the issues that destroyed his cool demeanor was when someone messed with his food. Before Mom could even swallow the fry, Ronnie exploded. "I asked you several times if you wanted fries and you said no. I would have bought you fries, so why are you eating mine?" Mom was completely shaken by this outburst from him and for the rest of the trip she never took another morsel of food from him. She had gotten the message loud and clear.

Nursing Home

When her health began to fail, Mom needed more help. It was decided that Mom should go to a local nursing home. The transfer to a local nursing home was not as difficult as it could have been because Sandy worked there as a nurse and she would be able to see Mom often. Many of Mom's children, along with grandchildren were able to visit her.

When my daughter became pregnant for the first time, she, and I, along with my son-in-law, made a weekday trip to let Mom know the good news. We brought some chicken and went to the dining room to eat it and tell her the news. The dining room was empty as the resident's at eaten earlier. As we told Mom about my daughter's pregnancy, she shouted for joy. She stopped anyone passing in the room to tell them, "I'm going to be a great-grandma." What was so remarkable to us was her jubilation. As of this time, she already had at least 20 great-grandchildren. She made my daughter feel like this baby was going to be her first great-grandchild. She did that with all her grandchildren. Each great-grandchild was a delightful and important addition to her family.

Sandy decided to take another job at a nursing home in Coldwater, Michigan which was about 30-45 miles from Jackson. Before long, Mom decided that she did not like being at the Jackson facility and wanted to go to Coldwater. Part of the reason for this decision was that the Jackson facility did not separate the dementia residents. Mom would wake up in the middle of the night to have a dementia patient standing over her bed shouting profanities at her. When this happened, she told me, "I am not afraid as I know they don't mean it. They are sick, but it does upset me."

I asked if she would like to go check out the facility in Coldwater where Sandy worked, and she thought that was a good idea. After looking at this facility and all that it had to offer, Mom told me she would like to move there. Some of my sibling's resisted this move as it was going to be further for them to travel to see her. After a couple of weeks, I asked her if she wanted to move, and her answer was, "no." I was totally surprised as she had really liked the Coldwater facility. I asked her why she had changed her mind and she replied, "I don't want to be the reason for any conflict among my children." I was amazed at the depth of love she had for all of us that she would stay in a place that was less than ideal just so there would not be dissention among her children.

Finally, after a few months, she just could not stand it any longer in Jackson and we decided to move her to Coldwater. She was happy there and she decided it was going to be her home.

❧

Dianne, Darlene, and I took turns making a Saturday trip to Coldwater to visit with Mom, take her out for a drive, and take her for lunch. I remember one time I arrived and on my way to her room, I was stopped by nurses several times who suggested various restaurants where I could take my Mom. I thought it was strange that they would give me all these suggestions. When I arrived in Mom's room, she had a smirk on her face, and asked, "Do you have any new lunch suggestions?" I told her, "No and why were all the nurses giving me suggestions on where we should go to lunch.". She confessed, happily, "I set them up to do this." Even in her old age, Mom still had that mischievous spirit.

Another time, I was sitting on Mom's bed trying to get her to decide what she wanted for lunch. Rather than name a restaurant, I asked her about food choices. i.e., Chinese, fried egg, liver and onions, a hamburger, etc. When there was a pause in our discussion, I heard a male voice shouting from a room down the hall, "I vote for liver and onions." Because she did not hear well, I had to speak very loudly, and he had heard our entire conversation.

Another incident with her hearing was when her one and only hearing aid was being repaired, and she could barely hear. I took her to a restaurant. They sat us in a section where five or six more tables were occupied. While we ate, I had to talk very loudly so she could hear. After a short time, I noticed that patrons were leaving and after they left the hostess was not seating any new guests in our section. By the time we left, we were the only ones in the section.

My daughter and I went to see Mom and take her out for dinner. We decided to really treat her and take her to an expensive restaurant. There were not many opportunities for her to experience a fancy restaurant. The three of us were seated close to another table. Even with her hearing aids we still had to speak loudly.

After we had ordered, the next table received a scrumptious chocolate dessert. Mom decided to tell us about an intestinal problem she was having. We tried to get her to speak softly, but to no avail. We were absolutely mortified. Mom just kept talking and was totally oblivious to the anxiety surrounding us. It was not long before the couple paid their check and quickly left the restaurant.

Because Mom did not sleep well at night, she enjoyed sleeping in. This was disconcerting for the nursing aides, as it complicated their schedule. They would go to Sandy and complain, "Your Mom won't get up for breakfast and let us help her get dressed. What do you want us to do?" Sandy would always reply, "Let her sleep. Do you know how many years she had to get up at the crack of dawn to fix breakfast for nine people?" From that time on the nursing aides let Mom sleep. Mom knew that whenever she woke up, she could get a hot cup of coffee in Sandy's office. As soon as Mom was dressed, she would head off in her wheelchair to get her coffee.

One day a corporate meeting was underway in Sandy's office when Mom wheeled herself in. Noticing the large group of well-dressed people, she said, "Don't mind me, I can't hear anyway. I just need a cup of coffee." Of course, everyone laughed and teased Sandy about this for a long time.

Carolyn J. Smith

On one occasion I took Mom to see her oldest and dearest friend, Opal. Opal was also in a nursing home about 30 miles away. Because of the distance and both of their health restrictions, they had not seen each other in many years. It was truly delightful to sit and watch these two old saints together once again. They thought of each other as good friends and most of all "sisters in Christ."

It was a little difficult for me during this visit as neither one of them could hear well, even with hearing aids. I had to repeat every comment each one made. At one point, Mom leaned towards Opal and said, "How are you doing?" Opal replied, "What?" Mom answered, "That's nice."

When we left, they both were delighted and thrilled to have been able to spend time together. That was the last time they saw each other.

On Christmas Eve day, I would go to Coldwater, load Mom and her suitcase into the car around noon so she could be with me on Christmas when most of the family would come over. We would stop at Dad's grave and place a Christmas wreath. Then we would go to my church for an early Christmas Eve service. I had to watch her closely when they distributed candles for everyone and lit them as she was not very stable, and I was fearful that she would burn herself, or set the church on fire. Once church was over, we would go to my house where my husband was making Christmas Eve dinner.

We always had Mom's favorite, which was shrimp, and lobster tail. Mom did not have many teeth, but she was able to enjoy the flavor. She would take a bite of some lobster or shrimp and move it around in her mouth to get as much of the juice and flavor out of it as possible. Once she had consumed all of the flavor, she would secretly, or so she thought, take the shrimp or lobster meat out of her mouth and lower her hand to feed it to the dog, who was waiting patiently at her feet. Our dog had a better meal on Christmas Eve than most people.

The day after Christmas I would take her back to Coldwater. She was ready to go back home. She was tired from all the family "chaos." When we reached the nursing home, I wheeled her into the lobby, where she shouted out, "Hey everyone, I'm home." It was home to her and she loved it.

Everyone loved her there, especially the staff. She was one of the most cheerful residents and they loved caring for her. I was told that one time she had had an accident and needed to be cleaned up. The aide felt awkward and Mom was embarrassed. So, what did Mom do, she started singing our high school fight song to alleviate the tension. It worked! Both she and the aide began laughing.

❧

Mom was always nice to everyone; however, she felt some resistance to her by some of the other residents. She felt the other residents were jealous of her because they thought she got special treatment due to Sandy working at the facility. She did get special treatment because everyone liked taking care of a fun and kind person.

Whenever she would see a new resident, she would go over and introduce herself and start a conversation with this person. She would tell me about the new people she met and those that she was able to lead to Christ. What a role model for the rest of us. Even at 91 years old, she was winning souls to Christ.

Smith Family Singers

Whenever we were together when I was young, we always sang. We especially sang when we were all crammed into our one and only car headed off to Battle Creek to visit Grandma for Sunday dinner. During this boring nearly two-hour ride, it was not long before someone started singing. Mom sang the lead along with the younger ones and Gloria and Darlene each sang their own harmony. Dad would add his baritone voice to this melodic sound. Mom's love of music was passed down to her children, grandchildren, and great-grandchildren. Everyone loves to sing!

I used my karaoke machine and sang in my basement many times during the week. When Mom was in assisted living, I asked if she would like me to come and sing for the residents. She thought that was a grand idea and was excited about showing off her daughter to the others. I called the administration office and made the arrangements for a date to sing. Mom could hardly wait. Before I started singing, I introduced myself as the daughter of Virginia Smith and had my Mom wave to everyone so they would know who she was in this group of about 50 people. In the days after I had been there, many residents whom she had yet not met came up to her and said, "Aren't you the one whose daughter came to sing for us?" Mom always replied proudly, "Yes, I am" and then a conversation would begin. She became a celebrity and loved it.

When she moved to another facility, she asked me to come and sing. She knew that once I came to sing, she would get noticed by the other residents. True to her personality, she always had a plan. At this point, a couple of my nieces joined me and as time went on, more and more family members joined the group. Mom was thrilled that this group included not only her children, but also almost all her grandchildren and great-grandchildren. Sometimes, there were more of us than there were residents. While we sang, the two and three-year old kids would be allowed to dance or play. The residents loved watching their antics. The songs were not always perfect, and some mistakes were made, but we had fun and the residents enjoyed listening to us and watching the little ones. Mom, most of all, loved singing with us, and we made sure to include her favorite songs. The smile on Mom's face, along with the other residents' smiles always made it worth the effort to take the time to do this. Some of our family travelled quite a distance, but because they loved Mom, they made the sacrifice.

A memorable moment in this ten-year period came when Fred, a resident of Coldwater, decided to join our group. We gave him the microphone so he could sing with us. Mom was a little jealous, but she understood that Fred did not have any family who came to visit him, and he needed us. The nursing home staff would put the date of our performance on the monthly calendar. Once it was published, Fred came rushing up excitedly to Mom to let her know that we were on the schedule, and he was looking forward to helping me sing. This statement was difficult for Mom to swallow. She really wanted to tell Fred that Carolyn does not need any help, but she restrained herself. She was perfectly confident in the knowledge that we came because we loved her, and she was also willing to share us with those less blessed.

Compassion

Compassion for others was one of my mother's most important attributes. This came about because of her close relationship with God. She understood completely that to love God was to love your neighbor. She always had a willing spirit to help someone, to feed someone, or just to show her Godly love to someone.

One of my fondness memories is when we were out to lunch and she asked if I would help her with something important she wanted to do. Of course, I said yes. She told me that one of her favorite aides was going back to her homeland in Venezuela to visit her 90-year old grandmother. Mom felt it would be nice to send along one of the angels she had been collecting to give to the grandmother. She thought this grandmother would like to have something from the United States.

We stopped at the store to pick up a gift bag, tissue paper and a card to go along with it. When we returned to her room, I asked her to pick out which angel she wanted to give away. This was a difficult choice for her. She wanted to send the perfect angel. Her thoughtfulness reminded me of the story in the Bible about the *widow's offering*. Mom had nothing materialistic to her name except this inexpensive angel collection, yet she was willing to give part of it away. What a blessing and lesson for me to witness.

"As Jesus looked up, he saw the rich putting their gifts into the temple treasury. He also saw a poor widow put in two very small copper coins. "Truly I tell you," he said, "this poor widow has put in more than all the others. All these people gave their gifts out of their wealth; but she out of her poverty put in all she had to live on." Luke 21:1-4 NIV

When Dad was alive, he took care of planting the graves on Memorial Day. After he passed, my daughter and I, and soon my two grandsons, took up the mantel for this task. We bought a carload of flowers, picked up Mom and took her to the two cemeteries where family members were buried. As we planted the

flowers, Mom sat in the front seat with the door open and told us stories of those buried here.

One grave she always made sure we planted flowers on was that of my grandmother's sister, Nettie. The story was that she died in childbirth and her husband had remarried. Neither he nor his children ever put anything on her grave. This fact saddened Mom, so she asked if we could be sure and plant this grave also. To this day, we look forward to planting the graves every year as it is a way to honor Mom, Grandma and Great-Grandma (GG).

Pearls of Wisdom

ven though Mom never graduated from high school and did not attend any college courses, she was full of wisdom. She spoke from her heart and what she felt God would be pleased with.

When I was about 12 years old, I was invited to attend a friend's birthday party. The party included a trip to the movie theater and then back to her home for ice cream and cake. I had never been to a movie theater before. My parents believed that it was sinful to attend a movie. This may seem odd today, however, back then we were being raised strictly the way our Pastor was interpreting the Bible.

I did not get many invitations to birthday parties and really wanted to go. I asked Mom if she would give me permission to attend the party, knowing that I would be going to the theater. She did not make the choice for me, but said, "It is your decision, however, what will you do if the Lord returns and finds you sitting in a theater?" She was giving me an opportunity to strengthen my own relationship with Christ and decide what I thought He would want.

I thought about it for a couple of days and justified my decision to attend the party by believing He would not care. I went to the party and the theater. I did not enjoy the movie nor can I even tell you what it was about, because I kept looking around the theater to see if God was coming back. This taught me a lesson to listen to the prompting of the Holy Spirit; if I do not have peace, it probably is not God's plan for me.

⁕

There was a time when one of my siblings was battling alcoholism and was in the hospital. Both Mom and Dad had supported him and his family during this difficult time. Another sibling thought she knew how Mom and Dad should handle the situation and suggested strongly that Mom go talk tough to him and convince him to make God his "higher power." Mom considered the suggestion and replied, "If I do that and try to tell him what to do, I might be interfering in God's plan for his life." It was not long before he started working seriously on his problem and through *Alcoholics Anonymous* and God, he became sober for the last 40 years of his life.

I admire her restraint, because as a Mother I think that I can fix everything. My Mom had the wisdom to know only God can fix things.

⁕

Our family reunion was basically a potluck, everybody brought something. One family member also contributed money by leaving it on the dresser in the bedroom she stayed in. I felt uncomfortable about accepting this money and told my Mom how I felt about it. Mom told me with certainty, "Carolyn, you cannot cheat people out of a blessing." I have used this phrase many times since when people give me something out of heartfelt generosity.

Going Home

I n January 2005, we discovered that gospel singer Bill Gaither was coming to town. Mom loved his music and had watched his videos for many years. She watched the videos so often she felt like she knew him. We, her children decided we should buy tickets and take Mom. A couple of weeks before the scheduled event, I wrote a letter to Bill Gaither and explained how important his music was to my almost 92-year-old Mom. I explained how his music calmed her down when she felt anxious and brought her joy as well. I asked if it would be possible for her to meet him after the performance. His staff called me and invited all of us to

go backstage. When I told Mom that she was going to be able to meet him she could hardly contain her excitement.

Mom was not feeling particularly well the day of the performance; however, she would not allow herself

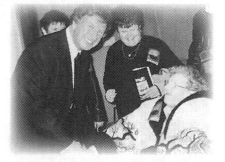

to miss out on meeting Bill Gaither. To Mom, Bill Gaither was a rock star. We enjoyed the entertainment, and directly after the concert made our way backstage with Mom in her wheelchair. When Bill came in the room, Mom did not realize it. Bill went to Mom, bent over in front of her taking her hands into his and said "Hello." Mom looked up into his eyes and exclaimed, "Bill, Bill, is it you?" He was so kind and gentle and spoke to her while she sat there weeping. As we were wheeling her out and before he went to another group, he called out to all of us and said, "Be sure and take care of her. She is special."

In February about 40 of the Smith Family Singers gathered at her nursing home to do our singing. Mom sat in her chair and enjoyed every song that was sung; however, she did not sing along with us as she usually did. We knew she did not feel well. The next weekend Dianne went to see her and reported to all of us that she did not look good. She was transported to the hospital where it was determined she had pneumonia in both lungs. Every day someone from our family came to visit her at the hospital. The medical staff determined that she could get the same care at the nursing home so Ronnie and his wife transported her back there.

Her condition was not really getting any better. With this news, Gloria decided to fly to Michigan to see Mom and say her goodbyes. When Gloria arrived in Michigan, I took the day off work and we drove to Coldwater to see Mom. She did not recognize us at first, but finally came around. After lunch we continued to sit in her room and sing hymns. She really was not very responsive, however, while we were singing the song *On Solid Rock*, and got to the chorus, Mom started to sing it with us as loud as she could. We were shocked!

We returned on Saturday with more family members. When it was time to leave, Gloria read her Psalm 23 and told Mom how much she loved her and what an inspiration she was to all of us. It was difficult to watch as the reality of Mom leaving this earth became evident.

Sunday, Monday, Tuesday, and Wednesday were all filled with visits to Mom. On Wednesday, the nursing staff recommended that we have hospice evaluate her. They did and determined she probably would not last more than 48 hours.

On Thursday morning, the 17th of March 2005, Ronnie, his wife, and Mom's cousin came to see her. In the afternoon ten of us arrived to gather around her. While we were there, Pastor Bob and his wife came to pray with Mom. We all knew what she would want and that was to hear us sing. We all started singing one Gospel song after the other. The harmony was beautiful. The other residents came out into the hallway to listen to us. One lady asked if we could come down and sing to her mom, as she was not doing well. We knew Mom would want us to do this, so we left Mom's room and went down the hall to sing to this other resident. We returned to Mom and continued singing. We could see that her breathing was beginning to be labored. I asked my daughter if she would sing the Gaither song that she learned for Grandma. She started singing it and we all joined in. While we were on the last line of the song, Mom took her last breath. The name of the song was, *I Know Who Holds Tomorrow*. It was a glorious ascension into heaven. The Director of the Nursing Home and the Nursing Director stood outside Mom's room during our singing and told us later that they had never witnessed such a peaceful passing.

During the visitation at the funeral home, her grandchildren gathered around her casket politely arguing over who was Grandma's favorite grandchild. It was delightful to watch them talk about the funny things she did. It was noted that many times she had been caught cheating at cribbage. The grandchildren secretly slid a cribbage board, along with a deck of cards into her casket where it would not be noticed. In memory of her cheating, one of them slipped a card up the sleeve of her garment. They were so proud of themselves and they knew their mischievous Grandmother, Ginge would have loved it.

❧❧❦

The funeral was held the following Monday at the Pentecostal Church which she had started attending 50 years earlier. There were three ministers that officiated, her great-granddaughter sang a favorite song of Mom"s, and seven or eight of her children and grandchildren spoke about how much they loved her and what she meant to them. The encounter with Bill Gaither was also part of her eulogy. On our ride to the cemetery, the number of vehicles that pulled over to the side of the road struck me. I had not seen this before and was moved by the fact that these strangers were honoring Mom. Throughout the funeral, I was reminded of a saying I once heard, "Those that live well, die well." While it was hard to let her go, she went out with celebration. I am sure she was watching the entire time and was pleased by the way that we honored her.

"Her children arise and call her
blessed...." Proverbs 31:28

Epilogue

My purpose in writing this account of my Mom's life is to demonstrate that it is not necessary to have self-confidence or a formal education, to impact the lives of others.

I trust you saw while reading this book that Mom influenced others without even knowing it. The way she treated people was not something she had to work at. It was who she was, engaging, entertaining, mischievous, compassionate, and joyful. The account of her life is filled with life-lessons.

I have felt her presence many times while writing, and I am sure that she is proud to have a book written about her. I am also certain that she feels unworthy of this honor. I tell her story with pride and to illustrate that no  matter what trials or tribulations we encounter, we can reach out to God for His power, strength, and love. Mom's belief was that if you made problem-solving secondary in your life of living close to God, you will find joy even in your most trying days. Mom taught all of us to believe this way, and she left us with a legacy of joy.

"I have told you this so that my joy may be in you and that your joy may be complete." John 15:11 NIV

About the Author

Carolyn J. Smith has always loved telling stories about events in her life. She especially loves to tell stories about her Mom, children and grandchildren, and recount stories about them.

Carolyn lives in a small town in Michigan and stays busy gardening, working at her part-time job, and singing with her Christian friends at various nursing homes.

Carolyn feels that one of the ways she can serve God is by telling stories of His provision, grace, and love in all areas of life. She has written three other books, *The Winter Season of My Garden, Let The Barren Sing and The Gift of a Christmas Cookie*.

If you would like to contact Carolyn, to get a copy of one of her other books, go to her Facebook page "Carolyn's Book Corner."

Printed in the United States
By Bookmasters